Kindness to Self,

and other mysterious superpowers

Healing the inner child,

and other myths of suppression

S. Caroline Hey

First edition November 2025
Book cover design by S. Caroline Hey
Edited by Martin Wale
Graphic support by Ahnjerin Art

Sydney, Australia
ISBN 978-1-7635010-4-1 (paperback)
ISBN 978-1-7635010-0-3 (eBook)
www.carolinehey.com

—

Other books by this author

Meditation for normal people,
and other not so woo-woo stuff

Off I Go... *from media to mindfulness*

Kindness to Self

This book is dedicated to my mother.
A woman I respect deeply.
A woman who tried hard to do all the right things.
Yet, fortunately, she "failed" many times.

She always surrendered to my quests and knew
better than to argue with me or try to talk me out of
them.
While witnessing how I healed my wounds,
she emulated me and investigated
what healing might mean for her.

Thank you mother, for always allowing me my space,
for never pushing me, never asking too many
questions, and always trying to learn from me.

Kindness to Self

It takes courage to be kind.

– Maya Angelou

Contents

—

Kindness to self

Loving Kindness meditation

Consequences

The freedom we gain

Bio-makeup

Forgiveness & ownership

Creation & curation

Kindness to Self

10

Introduction

Hi, and well done on following your impulse to buy this book. That seed of curiosity is very valuable. I look forward to growing with you. As the Yogic philosophy states, "always a teacher, yet forever a student." I hope you will have a great time reading, understanding, learning and maybe even starting to spread the word.
Let's start simple, shall we?

How are you doing?

"… *fine*?"

Right!? Let's try that again.

How are you really doing?
How is your heart?
Take a moment before you keep reading and sit with that question in honest contemplation.

The start of this book might be familiar. There is a reason for that. Keep reading to find out more.

Don't get me wrong, I am not asking you to sit there and desperately look for something that is not right in your life if you are in a good state.

What I am asking you to do, is to "look in the mirror" and investigate if "fine" is an accurate answer, or if a different word would be more appropriate.

If you have read my book *Meditation for normal people*, you'll recognize this question, and you might have added some words to your vocabulary in response to this question.

If not, go check it out.

This book, *Kindness to Self*, is another of the educational books I've written. My mission is to create easy introductions to becoming a better version of Self; to learn to understand yourself a little better, to learn and understand how your past affects your present. Reading and learning from this book will serve your friendships, partnerships in business and intimate relationships, and it might even help you solve long-standing family confrontations.

If the word **discomfort** makes you flinch, then you might not be ready for the journey. And that is okay too.

All my books are about expanding the narrative we live within. All my books come with a degree of discomfort, for some of you more than for others.

Sitting in discomfort is not something we get taught in life. Generally, everything in the Western world is built around avoiding discomfort. The "white man" has been ruled by his "monkey mind" for hundreds of years. During that time, the white man managed to dismantle many tribal cultures alongside.

Why?

Because the lives of the others were different and evoked discomfort in the white man. Instead of trying to understand the tribal cultures, we have tapped into suppression and oppression, and simply diminished different cultures just so the white man doesn't have to sit with their discomfort.

Funny, in the years 2020+, more than ever, people are seeking and aligning with tribal lifestyles.

Not only because we can, but more so because we seek. Travelling to foreign countries allows Westerners to find a non-Western lifestyle, to feel whole again.

Why is that?
When looking at why the brain avoids discomfort, we quickly realize it might not serve us anymore in the modern world. Fundamentally, the brain is built to avoid discomfort to save our lives. About 50,000 years ago, discomfort was sleeping on the prairie instead of in a cave, being exposed to danger instead of resting in safety.
Well, none of that is relevant anymore. We have (most of us) a safe home, food, and water.

So why is Western humanity looking for the tribal approach if we are supposedly safe?
To explain the paradox we find ourselves in, we are looking into the systematics of the human brain and what it's evolved into. It makes sense. We cannot blame white men entirely for acting upon these notions.

Back in 1800 we still very much, even as white men, had the community. A village, a generational household, the army, the church, you name it. Community and connection were strong.

However, in the 21st century, the community in Western culture has largely died out. We are digitally more connected than ever, yet our sense of real connection is dwindling away.

Discomfort in the 21st century is a too hard bed, a broken chair, a rainy day at the bus stop – nothing life-threatening.

On the flip side, discomfort can be growth, widening our awareness of Self and the world that we inhabit. Discomfort is looking in the mirror and seeing where we must make changes.

Changing the world, instead of the Self, might have worked (on an unhealthy and damaging scale) a few hundred years ago. But in 2020+, it really is all about the individual needing to look at themselves.

If you are still with me, great!

Let's become a little uncomfortable, let's grow and maybe even heal.

Who am I to write this book?

I am Caroline Hey, Dip. Cert. Med. Somatic Trauma Therapist, and 10+ years mindfulness practitioner. Since mindfulness found me, the first decade has been a steep learning curve. I've been through multiple levels of hell and back. Mindfulness has saved my life at least three times, in the most literal sense.

Those struggles and life-altering events came with the necessity of learning to listen, evaluate, reframe, readjust, change; being exposed to a ton of discomfort, and starting over, and over, and over again.

Amongst all those start overs, I was protected by some higher force. I call it faith, you might call it God, others call it whatever resonates with them.

My trust in something beyond has led me to meet kindred spirits who guided me toward these new directions. Directions of healing, overcoming, learning new tools, and eventually understanding my calling and discovering my purpose.

To no surprise, it has always been within me, I just didn't understand it. I wasn't kind enough to myself to really tune in to what my innermost Self was made for.

All of the above led, over time, to going back to school and a stark career change. Here I am, having become a teacher, healer, and guide for many – yet I remain a student, forever evolving, learning, and healing along the way.

In all my books, before starting to delve deeper into the matter, I put out one disclaimer and ask one question.

Disclaimer:
Once you start the work, it's impossible to stop.

Question:
I ask you to be fully honest with yourself. With all the cards out on the table, are you ready to change your life?

Starting to heal old patterns and entering the world of mindfulness takes courage and is a choice you make that will shape everything from here moving forward.

Like a big fat pink elephant that you cannot unsee. If your answer is no, well good on you for recognizing it, and I thank you for reading all the way to this point. I encourage you to flick the book forward to someone else instead of just abandoning it.

If your answer is yes, welcome to the journey.
I promise to use words that resonate, explain vocabulary, teach gently, and make clear when anecdotes are stemming from personal experiences, which can or will highly differ from your own experiences to come.

Kindness & stress

The problem with kindness is, it's a circular motion. If people are not kind to us, we don't know what kindness is. That manifests in not being kind to ourselves, which then reflects into the world, and we are not kind to others either.

Input–resonance–output.

Now, think about how you have been talked to at home and at school when you were a child. Let's say between the ages of 4 and 16 years old. Anything before 4 years old matters too, but you won't be able to remember it.

As a child, naturally, we do not have the life experience and comprehensive understanding of the Self which we do as an adult. That means, if parents are busy or short with us, we perceive their behaviour as a "punishment" and infer we are not good enough. Not because our parents don't love us, they probably do. But their world is full of other stuff. They forget how narrow the world is for little kids.

Take a moment and reflect on your own shortcomings with friends or co-workers when you are stressed. Given that you otherwise have a great relationship with them. If you snap at them or you decline a dinner invitation, they know you have not "fallen out of love" with them. They understand you are simply under stress.

However, as a child, you do not have that background information. As a 7-year-old, you don't know what stress is. You can feel it, and it's scary because it makes the adults in your world go bananas. But you don't know that it is not related to you.

What is stress?
Stress is a hormonal reaction to circumstances. When people refer to stressors, the vocabulary used is often incorrect. Stress isn't a physical thing happening to us. Stress is a reaction to an overload of input.

That input is either; too high in intensity in too short an amount of time, or beyond what we can tolerate over a prolonged period. Stress is the little sibling to trauma.

Noteworthy, kids are not stressors, they are activators, commonly referred to as "triggers".

Let's make that relatable for an adult. Say you have a full day of meetings and all of a sudden you get that one eMail that needs to be addressed right then and there. The eMail is the trigger, not a stressor. The eMail didn't do anything, it is just an eMail. However today, in the example given, it is the "straw that breaks the camel's back".

The eMail contains a deadline, or a major fuck up that only you can fix. But, you also have the next meeting in less than 5 minutes. Your body recognizes the signals of urgency. And this time conflict becomes, for us, the trigger. Film, media and society have "trained" our brains in what triggers are.

Here you are, with your well-trained brain recognizing a trigger. You have no choice (you do, but we get there later) other than to release stress hormones.

One of the most commonly known and fundamentally the most relevant hormone related to stress is cortisol.

What is this cortisol anyway?

Cortisol is a hormone. Before all the men in the room pretend they are not "hormonal", sorry to break it to you, you have hormones too. In fact, men have more than women, testosterone is one of them. The reasons for that could fill a whole other book. For now, let's stick to why we have cortisol and what it does.

The hormone cortisol gets released by the two adrenal glands sitting on top of your kidneys. The pituitary gland in the brain regulates cortisol production. That means your brain is heavily involved in the stress response because it's the original source of the signals to release cortisol.

What does cortisol release do? It basically releases stored sugars and gets our blood rushing, by making our heart pump faster, which then increases blood flow to our brain. Our brain now has the ability to make decisions fast.

However, the brain is **lazy** at the same time and doesn't worry about getting that fast-moving blood all the way to the prefrontal cortex (PFC).

Think of an old water-mill wheel. The wheel rotates with the least resistance in one direction only. The brain works in a similar way, it moves all that fast-rushing blood to the shortest access points – the back-center and lower brain structure – anything that keeps vital organs and the reactive center intact. That means the front of the brain is undersupplied.

The front of the brain, literally the part that sits behind your forehead, above your eyes, is the prefrontal cortex. The PFC is responsible for planning for the future, looking for the comfortable things in life, and envisioning.

Unfortunately, the brain doesn't think that the PFC is relevant during stress and stops the blood flow about halfway.

So the majority of the blood rushes into the back of the head. The part that sits just above the neck. The lower brain stem, often called the primal brain.

That part of the brain, as the name reveals, is old-school and primal, and all about "survival".

Your visual window decreases – you physically see less environment in your peripheral vision – and you only see straight ahead with laser focus. Your muscles tense, and your digestive and reproductive systems slow down. You are in reaction mode, not in response mode.

Long-term stress means you are putting your body in a constant state of fight or flight mode. These persistently increased cortisol levels lead to the immediate correlation of gaining weight, reduced sex drive and tension.

Let's look at our earlier scenario again.

You see the eMail, the eyes send the information to the brain for processing, brain connects to memory of schedule.

Memory says the schedule is full for the day, brain perceives time conflict as a threat and reacts by gearing up to overdrive producing stress. Brain sends signals to adrenal glands to release stress hormones, blood rushes to the brain for faster thinking but narrows the solution focus option. You freak out, sweat, and your breath shortens. Your tummy knots, your thighs tighten, and your hands struggle to grip small, fiddly objects.

Fine motor skills are impaired, while gross motor skills kick in. You take bigger steps, move faster, grip harder, and speak louder.

Self-love and care for others decrease or deactivate.

It all makes sense from 50,000 years ago. If you're being chased by a lion in the wilds of Africa and running for your life, giving yourself a hug and singing Kumbaya probably isn't the right move. And you're not planning your future right then. If anything, your past rushes before your eyes.

It's a nightmare.

I am stressed just writing about it.

What does any of the above have to do with kindness?

Everything.

Where does kindness fit in here?

If right then, in that eMail scenario above, a calm person walks into the room and says something nice – best case you do not even hear it. Worst case, it's yet another trigger of stress and you snap "Shut up!" Which is far away from kindness. If we are untrained, we cannot be kind when in a hyperactive state.

Following is a scenario perceived by a child.
A girlfriend of mine shared a story with me during one of our catch-ups. Her 5-year-old boy has tendencies of anxiety when schedules change in his life, for example when his swimming class was moved from 6 p.m. Wednesday to 8 a.m. Saturday.

There are multiple factors we should look at as a parent.
First, what is his personality type? Is the boy's bio-astrological makeup (see Bio-makeup chapter) an unstable or stable personality?

Depending on that makeup, parents can approach conversations with their kids in a way that resonates with their kids and makes them feel safe. A parent will need to learn their child's "language."

Second, he is the younger sibling of two. The older sibling is a girl. That means it's not the first rodeo for the parents and they are placing an unconscious expectation and comparison upon the kids, who are not only different age groups, but different genders too.

Third, what else is changing too frequently in this little human's life that may cause him to feel unstable within change? That is the point where we, as therapists, look at the broader life routine. As humans, especially parents, we need to understand that to a child, routines can seem like hairy, scary monsters under the bed. Parents need to explain routines rather than just establishing and enforcing them upon a child without a conversation of the greater good, such as safety and stability.

Again, it's all about perception, experience and language.

Little ones compute experiences differently from adults. Routine can be scary, especially when never explained why they need it. For them it's just a "thing" they need to do. What they perceive and train their brain is – if we don't follow that routine, love is sacrificed, and Mom and Dad get mad.

After some dialogue, my girlfriend suggested that when her boy is showing discomfort about something in life, which in a rational sense means he is feeling unsafe, his dad shuts the boy down. Dad might be like the person having received the eMail in scenario one. Being stressed, he snaps at the boy along the lines "Get over it." Dad is totally lacking kindness because he is stressed with something else.

The little boy is now exposed to his father's stress reaction. The boy's brain is learning what stress means and starts programming by monitoring the physical reaction evoked by Dad's comment – discomfort, sadness, uncertainty, lack of love, lack of worthiness, and disconnection.

Intuitively, the little boy knows he is a boy. He knows he is the same "thing" as Dad, just smaller. His brain computes, "What Dad does is right, and I need to do so too."

The words are irrelevant when one is 5 to 8 years old. He doesn't "hear" the words his dad is saying. The boy only sees and feels his dad's tension and withdrawal.

Dad is not a bad dad, but Dad has forgotten how a little boy's landscape is shaped. Dad has forgotten that kids are absorbing action over words. Kids learn based on "monkey see, monkey do".

In this case, Dad has it particularly hard to be a good role model. Dad was adopted as an infant. Therefore he has no memory of his first lack of care or disappointment, but his brain and body remember it all.

As very small kids, we have no language to understand what bodily sensations mean.

But it's all stored in the bio-makeup. His adoptive parents surely did a great job. Yet there will forever be that visceral memory of detachment and re-attachment.

Later, Dad served in the US military in the Middle East. For Dad, "keeping it together" and "sucking it up" meant life or death in the war zone for him and his comrades. For Dad, it was a trained survival mechanism.

In fact, Dad is a great human being able to live through a crisis, because he'll keep his "shit together". As a wife, you want someone like that to be the leader of the family. Yet, Dad will have to get unstuck from his battleground narrative to function in the "normal" world. There are no "enemies" hiding around every corner. Your friends will not drop dead because you've forgotten to bring the carton of beer to the Sunday BBQ.

Re-entering "real life" after military service is unfortunately not well done by any government body, and often leaves families in conflict. Some more than others. Unlearning and reprogramming the stress response is key to becoming a better, kinder human. Kindness is something we can learn, relearn and regain at any age or stage of life. The beauty is, it is very tangible and at times should be made more visible.

To sum up the above, Dad has to learn to breathe through stressors and triggers.

Dad needs to reprogram himself that his boy is not a trigger, and has to be met with kindness at all times. In addition both parents need to become more verbal and explanatory about schedules, priorities, and discipline.

How to make kindness visible

Changing one's language in the middle of a sentence shows people you're proactively learning. That will trigger more kindness and softening in the language of others too, like a ripple effect. I talk about the ripple effect a lot in my books.

Whenever you start a sentence and, halfway through, you realize it will not quite come out the way you intended it to sound, just stop. Take a brief pause, and say,

"Let me rephrase that." and start over.

This is particularly impactful to children, as they are hearing and **feeling** the full process, including a safe change of attitude.

Let's say we had good and well-spoken parents, but school was challenging. Kids were teasing you, maybe even teachers were being inappropriate. That sends mixed messages to a kid and creates two separate narratives during their upbringing. It may support a change of behavior, for example becoming introverted.

If there is never any conflict at home, but constant conflict in school, one will naturally retreat within themselves – their safe space – and not engage with the outer world. The outer world is conflicting.

If the dynamics of both environments are rough and lack kindness – like in my personal experience – then one can only hope that the bio-astrological makeup is in your favor, to always lead you back to being curious. Being curious and not accepting the "bad" in the world, and to keep searching for the "good" till we find it, is a superpower.

However, in many unfortunate cases, a continued exposure to a lack of kindness can lead in the other direction.
Trauma.
I won't go into the subject of trauma in this book, as there is a full book in this series dedicated to a trauma-informed approach in life.

As you can see, kindness is a damn big deal and really should be taught as a subject from kindergarten through to high school.

How to be kind

If kindness is a rather foreign concept for you, start with the outer world first. We usually struggle most to be kind to ourselves. Baby steps are recommended.

Here are some examples:
When buying your coffee, leave the counter by wishing the person who served you a nice day.
At the supermarket start using a service check-out instead of the self-check-out.
Say thank you more often, even for the little things. You'll be amazed how many surprised looks you will get. You will literally make their day, make them feel seen, give them a chance to pay that kindness forward.
This is the ripple effect I referred to earlier.

Return to old-fashioned values like holding the door open for someone, asking visibly lost people if they need some directions, or simply smile at a stranger when your eyes meet.

But – to see those things, to recognize these moments, one must be aware!

Open your eyes.

Put your phone away.

Sit once a week in a cafe or on the commute to work and **not** use your phone. Simply observe the world around you. You will find incredible beauty hidden in everyday life.

Next time you are in a bad mood or something goes wrong at work, force yourself to stop. Look at yourself and at the words rushing through your mind.

Are your words reaffirming what just went wrong? "Damn, I'm so stupid.", "I really fucked that one up, didn't I?", "Everyone always blames me, Jon Doe never gets called out on his stupid shit.", "What kind of an idiot am I?"

Not the best conversations to have with Self, are they? Let's try to stop those words from coming.

It is a fact that motion creates emotion. Next time you catch yourself with these negative voices in your head, literally move away from them.

If you are walking, stop and if space permits, take a step to the **left** side and say out loud "[Your name], stop, don't talk like that.

You are better than that." Replace the negative words with words of affirmation and growth, and start walking again at a slightly different pace.

For example, "Next time I'll do better." or "Clearly there is room for me to learn more."

"Why am I triggered like this?" or "This person might have something going on in their life, but I am not allowing them to affect mine."

If you are sitting somewhere and your head is running away with itself, and you catch yourself with negative self-talk – get up, turn away from the chair and say out loud "[Your name], stop, don't talk like that. You are better than that.", then turn the chair around before sitting on it to continue with your task.

If these options seem inappropriate or simply aren't possible, just stop for a moment and take at least three deep breaths. **Yes, I mean that.** It is more than an old wives' tale.

Breathe in through the nose to the count of 4, out through the mouth to the count of 6.

If you are in public, simply adjust your posture. Plant both feet firmly on the ground – whether you are sitting or standing – and look for the furthest point you can see.

Keep or make your spine straight and tall, imagining a puppet string pulling you up from the top of your head. Lift your shoulders towards your ears, roll them back, then pull them down to release tension. Then say to yourself, "[Your name], don't talk like that. You are better than that." Remain in that upright, stable position for at least three cycles of natural breath.

Eventually, start introducing positive language into your day without the need of a prompt. If speaking kindly to yourself is too hard, write on your bathroom mirror with a marker, instead.

Pick one personalized quote, or any of the following affirmations:

"I am enough."
"I am a good human."
"I am smart."
"I am love."

Maybe change your phone screen to a quote, or put an alarm on your phone 10 minutes after a meeting you were unsure about. Let the alarm read "I am enough." or "I did well."

Kindness, like many things, grows like a muscle. The more we exercise it, the better we get, and eventually it can become a habit. People will start referring to you as the kind person in the room, or even in their lives.

The thing with kindness is, you can only win.

Healing & modern-age charlatans

A dictionary definition:
Healing [Hee'ling] The process of the restoration of health. With physical trauma or disease suffered by an organism, healing involves the repairing of damaged tissue(s), organs and the biological system as a whole and resumption of (normal) functioning. Health is not the mere absence of disease.

Healing, a word thrown around loosely since 2020, during and after the global pandemic.
All of a sudden, social media "influencers" are "healers", "breath-work specialists", "yoga teachers" or other modern charlatans promising a better life if you follow their accounts. These self-proclaimed "healers" are popping up like mushrooms to a sickening level of saturation. It is a **dangerous** world out there. The stage is a very different one from that of previous centuries – more global and accessible due to various social media channels – yet the charlatans haven't changed much.

The louder their claim, the less likely their knowledge is real, or their intentions are pure. As trained allied-health practitioners, we take an oath to help those in need and to put support before personal benefit. I am not saying one should not make a living with their gift — I do so too — however, shouting all the flash words from the rooftops, without backup knowledge or broader support for the times when things go wrong, is immoral at best and dangerous at worst. It can leave the participants with more trauma than they had when they first walked in. Many professional practitioners are questioning the true intentions of the "anti" social-media charlatans.

My accountant keeps telling me that all the trauma caused by untrained Instagram influencers is good for my business. Well, she is not wrong. However, that is not how I want the world to go around. I don't want people to get scarred by attending a new-age wanna-be's breath-workshop or EMDR (Eye Movement Desensitization and Reprocessing) weekend course. These tools are very effective!

But if provided without the proper training, they will leave the participants in an upset state. I didn't train as an allied—health practitioner to become instead an emergency "trauma paramedic" fixing weekend warriors. Yet that seems to be what my most recent inquiries are mounting up to.

It's a sad paradox. I love seeing the increase in people wanting to experience alternative pathways to healing their stress, traumas, and misalignments.

However, before you attend any workshops that promise a "quick fix", do your research. Enquire about the provider's training certificate and experience portfolio.

Your mental health depends on it!

I became a practicing therapist to proactively heal my clients and readers, and support them in resolving trauma. At a later stage, while working together, that may entail a holistic approach of therapy. Which through my network embraces other modalities such as EMDR, hypnosis, meditation, or breath—work. This network of allied—health practitioners is a close—knit circle of trained and experienced facilitators who are registered and fully certified.

One of my most recent clients came to me after attending an afternoon "circle" of breath-work facilitated for 45 people by 1 guide. That rings all the alarm bells. No practitioner will be able to hold a **controlled** session for 45+ people. That is incredibly dangerous.

Breath-work taps into our deeply stored experiences of emotional, physical and spiritual misalignment. It is an amazing tool, and I use it too when needed.

It unleashes a deep, suppressed level of wounding. However, when done on a larger scale and without proper integration – integration is the key component here – it can leave you extremely unbalanced, irritated, and can lead to depression. At the end of the charlatan's version of breath-work, they send you home with no integration roadmap or contact, to work with what came up. You are left alone with your newly surfaced memory to work through what has come up. Now, you not only have to deal with this new piece of information, you also have to find a trusted practitioner to help you deal with it.

Yeah, good luck with that!

Interestingly, humans are less inclined to work preventively on self-care and are more proactive with healing only when shit hits the fan.

Healing is a journey we choose to embark on when we can no longer tolerate the pain.
Fortunately for us, we live in a Western society with a choice between doctors, therapists, approved alternative routes, books, podcasts, etc.
Don't get me wrong, I am not against investigating new avenues, otherwise you would not have found this book. What I am warning about is the legitimacy of the qualifications of those who put themselves out there.
My approach to the subject will not be everybody's cup of tea either.
In fact, I hope that people will question my legitimacy and do some digging to see if what I teach and practice serves their journey.

Communication & language

Language can be anything from body language, to expression, to gesture, signing, and more. It is culturally diverse, and can be emotionally influenced. So, how many different spoken languages do humans use?

Let's start with the big picture, and then zoom down, step by step, all the way to the language we use on a very personal level.

As of Feb 2024, the number of living languages spoken in the world varies depending on the source. Some state that there are 7,106 living languages, while others suggest that there are around 6,500 languages we speak as adults amongst our peers.

Now let's start zooming in a little, using English as an example, as this book is written in English. Acknowledged and recognized as first language English-speaking countries are North America, Britain, Ireland, South Africa, Australia, parts of Canada, the Caribbean Islands, Singapore, Hong Kong, and New Zealand.

Zooming in again, we have subdivided cultures, and newly English-adapted countries including – but not limited to – India, Papua New Guinea, Malta and many more.
Zooming in further. Within the English language, there are hundreds of accents and dialects alone. Dialects within the nations depend purely on the region. Texan, Yankee, Joburg, Outback Queensland, Geordie··· You get the gist of it.

Now zoom to the more personal level of how you speak to your peers? What is your work language? I bet it differs to that between your friends, family, sports club, spouse, children, and self-talk?

Becoming very personal now, zooming into a micro level. How do you speak to your Self? Rather kind, somewhat empowering, a little discouraging, pretty condescending, vaguely patronizing?
Finally, let's zoom right down to a nano-level, which you may have never realized till now, or you might have proactively avoided till today.

How do you speak to your pain, your challenges, your thoughts. And ultimately, how do you speak to your inner child?

Do you even address any of these vital matters at all on a conscious level?

I invite you to take out a piece of paper and write down the first 10 words that come to mind when you debate with yourself about a topic.

Let's say work was stressful, and a client or co-worker has hurt you with their approach and words. You have been aware enough of the hurt to remove yourself for 5 minutes and go outside or hide in the toilet. But at the end of the day, this hurt is still lingering.

What kinds of words are going through your mind right now? Is your list of words full of blame or full of claim? Are you coming from a lineage of patronization, or of compassion?

Blame/Patronization:
I am not worthy, I am a fool, I am a bad employee, I am not good enough, they are right, I should never have got this job, I might get fired, I probably should get fired, maybe I should quit, I deserve this, everyone is out to get me at all times anyway, etc.

Claim/Compassion:
I deserve to be here, I have knowledge, I am here to serve to the best of my ability, I am a good human, they must have had a bad day, I am not the problem, I am strong, I am calm, I am worthy of respect.
How can I improve from this, how can I learn from this, how can I maneuver through this better next time?

I am going to make a bold statement here and suggest that up to 80% of all readers of this book have a big **blame** list, and the minority have a dominating **claim** list.

Before we move on to the next chapter, take a moment to sit with that discovery. Have a think about how and where you can start being kinder to yourself. Try using positive and self-affirming language, protecting yourself from a downward spiral of feeling unqualified, inadequate, sad, unworthy, or worse.

Every human is born with a space to claim. Claim yours.

Childhood & other traps

First of all, there is no such thing as "one size fits all" when it comes to childhood. Our childhood experience is as unique as our fingerprint. Even if you are an identical twin and have had the "same" upbringing, you did not experience the same childhood. Perception is key here!

Every human is unique in the makeup of their brain matter, developmental stages of perception, intake of surroundings, sensitivity to sound, smell, taste, touch, etc.

If you are a pessimist, you might look at this as "We are doomed from the start". However, if you're an optimist, you might look at it with "Wow, so much to discover".

It's been doing the rounds for some time now that all our trauma lies within our childhood.

Well, let's stop right there. Trauma is a big word, and like many other words and phrases these days, it is greatly misused. As mentioned previously, there is another book in this series that looks more deeply into the trauma-informed approach.

So, please do not fret. Childhood's not all that bad when basing it on a "normal" upbringing. Though, normal can be an oxymoron in itself.

Let's meet on middle ground. Let's assume we had non-psychopathic parents and they genuinely tried hard to do their parenting to the very best of their ability, with the knowledge they had, and access to the information at hand.

Anybody old enough to read and understand this book in 2020+ has parents who may have had no, or limited, access to the internet or other resources on how to raise kids. Your parents likely acted based on their own experiences. Either because it was good, or it was not good and they tried a different approach.

No matter what your relationship with your parents is at this particular point in time, take a brief moment and give them recognition and respect for their efforts. A mental thank you.

There are as many scenarios of possible childhood experiences as there are humans in this world. When looking at it in hindsight, we are all able to see our childhood as unique and personal. Memories, good and not so good, can be triggered by sounds, smells, visual cues and touch. Our senses are the gateway to our memory bank.

Let's do an exercise.

Gently start backtracking to good memories. Pick any age and think of a moment full of joy. A moment that makes you smile. Perhaps, recall one or two such moments.

When you find a moment, "look around" and see who is there with you. Friends, family, pets, stuffed toys, no one? Then look further and look at what you are surrounded by. Nature, walls, day, night?

Write your moment/s down below. Make this your memory to come back to when other, less positive, memories surface.

_____

_____

_____

_____

Kindness to Self

_____
_____
_____
_____
_____
_____
_____
_____
_____
_____
_____
_____
_____
_____
_____
_____
_____
_____
_____
_____
_____
_____

(tear out page, keep for later)

Throughout the journey of this book, you might experience some long-forgotten memories resurfacing. Some of them will be good, others might be rather confronting.

Whenever you are ready, turn the page and let's awaken what is there.

The Inner Child, what even ...?

Okay, what exactly is the Inner Child?

Basically the inner child is, in the most literal sense, your "mini–me". When someone asks you about your favorite childhood memory, your brain is lightning fast (even faster than Google), skimming through every single experience stored in your "library". That library never closes from the moment you are born till the moment you die.

Unfortunately, sometimes due to illness, pathways to access the library can become blocked. Yet the library itself never closes. But the library has shortcuts too, your senses. A smell, a sound, a sight, a touch, a taste can evoke memories without using words or setting a scene. They just pop up based on the trigger/activator. You then respond somatically to a sensory memory.

Circle back to the memory I asked you to write down in the previous chapter. Your brain remembered the scene, and automatically brought up an age estimate and a version of Self. As an adult, you are able to look at that memory like a photograph.

You might remember as much as the temperature of the day (somatic response), the weather in general, what you wore, how your hair was, how the air smelled, and how you felt. The longer you sit in the memory, the clearer it becomes.

As an adult, you now have additional life experience and a level of judgment, a sense of fairness, morals and values. Your childhood memory interlaces with your adult knowledge. That makes it harder as an adult to fully enjoy childhood memories. Depending on the memory, you might giggle to yourself and follow up the thought with a degrading sentence such as, "It's silly that I liked this/did that." And nostalgia gets created.

No childhood memories, especially the good ones, are silly! It all made perfect sense and felt amazing at the time. Keep those memories clear, and that joy pure.

When beginning to work with your Inner Child, it's easiest to start first with a scenario, such as a friend's birthday party or a favorite vacation. Later, when we are more comfortable going back into the memory bank, we can take a direct route via sensations we felt.

Start very gently. First, have a look within yourself and understand what age you identify with as a child version of yourself. By law, we are classified as children from birth till the age of 18 in most countries around the world.

What age pops up for you when thinking of yourself as a child? There is no right or wrong answer.

I, for myself, have two versions of my mini-me. One of them is stuck in a particular scenario. She is 12 years old, always on her own in the same place when I connect with her. It's a real place in the town I grew up in, but in a deserted version. She sits on the bench in a tram shelter waiting for a tram. It's always the same surroundings, mini-me is wearing the same clothes, the streets are empty, the colors are blunt and filtered through a grey-yellow lens. A somber kind of mood. That version of me is struggling with self-worth, trust, being loved, and direction in life.

The second version of my inner child is the 6-year-old me. She is cute and innocent, she is looking for love and doesn't mean any trouble.
She isn't stuck in a particular scenario, and doesn't wear the same clothes in any given memory. She is free and cheeky at times. She is fun, but she isn't 100% real. Her name is also Caroline, however my name wasn't Caroline when I was 6 years old. That is interesting. Both versions are valid. They never both appear in the same "sitting". They come up when they feel the need to be seen, heard and healed.

When I first "met" them, it was both very empowering, and grief-stricken at the same time. By listening to "them" in separate visits, I have understood more about my adult self. It helped me to realize how I became me and why I struggled as a grown woman in certain areas of my life.

I have clients who are drawn to their 16-year-old Self, whilst others are drawn to a 9-year-old version. It's all about trust and surrender to allow the version to surface that most needs to be seen at the time of self-inquiry.

Whichever version first appears for you, it might not be the only one. We may have several mini-me's to heal.

Some versions will heal quickly, as the rationality of an adult brain can explain a scenario that was hurtful at the time, when we lacked a comprehensive understanding. You can have that trusting conversation with your mini-me that hadn't taken place back then. Explain to your mini-me the *why* and *what,* and the *how* of the situation. Be the support that was lacking at the time.

Another version of your inner child may need more work and might require help from a trained allied-health professional or psychologist. Many kids lack the feelings of trust and touch. Most clients lack being heard and seen throughout their lives. Parents were busy with work, or siblings, or social engagements.

When discovering in conversation with your inner child that absent parents were a problem, ask the questions, have a dialog with your mini-me, and allow yourself to go there.

Be gentle with yourself, allow movements and emotions. Watch what comes up.

Heat in your spine? Hands trebling? Heavy breathing? Tears welling up? The need to lie down? The need to self-soothe by gently rocking, holding your own hands, caressing your own body? There is no wrong engagement. There are no wrong feelings.

Enquire gently if it's fear, mistrust, shame, loneliness, worthlessness, curiosity, anger, or sadness. There is no wrong emotion.

The five "W's" are a great gateway for this exercise.

Why

What

Where

Who

Why

Yes, the **why** is there twice.

Meeting your inner child

To get in touch with your inner child, I recommend creating a space that is safe, warm, and familiar. Best case scenario is at home in a room that is less frequently used, or used to practice yoga or other slow movement. A room that has a calming effect on you.

You can use the bedroom. However, I'd suggest not using the bed, but creating a nook on the floor in the corner of the room. We do not want to mix the present with the past.

Let's say you are married with children. You do not want your bed to become the point of memory, as that will block you in your sexual endeavors moving forward.

You might want to lie on the floor in your kid's room when they are out of the house to recreate a child-like environment.

For the first time – or any other time for that matter – you might want to have the TV or radio on, or any other device playing music or providing a talking noise, in a different room from where you want to meet your inner child.

You are not actively listening, it simply serves as "white noise", something that resembles the effect of being at home as a child, with life happening outside your room.

You might want to start seated, maybe leaning against the bed or the wall. You might want to have something to fiddle with. If you still have a favorite toy you had as a child, please have that with you for its pacifying effect.

Start asking, out loud, which child would like to talk to you first. If it is your first time, invite your inner child to meet you halfway.

"Here I am, I am you. If you are here too, I'd like to meet you. Would you like to meet me halfway? You don't have to be afraid. It's safe. No one is here to judge you. I am here, ready when you are."

Take a deep breath and sigh it out. Close your eyes if you feel comfortable doing so. You might want to change your arm position and loosely hug yourself. One arm wrapped over the other in front of your body. You might feel inclined to sway or fidget. Let your body lead the way.

If you feel like curling up on the floor, please do so. Make sure it's comfortable, with pillows and blankets. You are here to soothe and create a safe space, to make sure whichever version is emerging feels welcome.

As a version, or scenario, or feeling starts building up before your inner eye, or within the fibres of your body, watch and observe.

Calling your inner child doesn't necessarily have to be a "real" memory, but a new story you can create for yourself. A secret place perhaps, that you fabricate in your mind, or a merging of true locations you have been to throughout your lifetime. Wherever feels safe, that's where you'll find your inner child.

Once you've seen **your** mini—me ,or sensed **your** mini—me, invite that energy closer. Build trust, and reassure them that you will cause no harm, that you are here to listen. Start by introducing yourself. Start with something around the lines, "Hi, how are you? I am you. I am [your name]. I am your adult you. I'd like to meet you. I am here to protect you."

Gently invite your inner child closer. Allow all the space your mini—me needs. It can take multiple visits from you to your mini—me to generate trust. For others, it might be fast, and your inner child is coming running towards you as if they were waiting for you.

Go into this experience with no expectations, but be open to all possibilities. If the scenario permits, hold your inner child, hug your mini—me, cradle them. Give your inner child the love you would have liked to receive back then, when this was you in the real world. When no one heard you, no one saw you.
If tears are flowing, simply allow them to fall. If singing or sounds are released, simply allow them out. If you fall asleep, simply allow it to happen.
For the first time in a long time, be you (now) with you (then).

After care, repetition & beyond

How often should you visit your inner child?
Once you have established a good connection with your inner child, you can visit your mini-me as much as you wish.
You might start to notice where their behavior patterns show up in your adult life as stressors, and you are now able to recognize them and change your responses, instead of blindly reacting. From here, you can initiate change and elevate the quality of your life.

Your inner child can become your "superpower" to navigate through adult life. Every time you show up for your mini-me, you can become for them that safe place you didn't have as a child, that voice to speak up for yourself when no one else did, and you start healing your inner child's wounds. This will result in you showing up differently in your current life.

Depending on your adult behavioral shortcomings, these will ease. If you were prone to anger, your short fuse will ease up. If you never spoke up for yourself, you will find your voice. If you were timid and shy, you will become more interested in engaging with people around you.

You are healing your past and simultaneously preventing the creation of more pain in the present. This will set you up for a more productive and less turbulent future.

Every time you "travel" to visit your inner child, make sure you drink lots of water that day and the following day. Working with energy is very tiring to the body. Do not drink alcohol or take drugs for 48 hours before or after your "meeting".

Do not set out to meet your inner child with the intention of revisiting a severely traumatizing event. If you believe you have severe trauma, and you are scared to go there, just don't. Look for a facilitator who is reputable, a trained and recommended allied—health professional who specializes in dealing with trauma and trauma resolution.

There is no specific rhythm for how often these exercises should be repeated. You might do it once and decide it's not for you at this point in your life. And that is okay.

Or, you might want to resolve an issue at hand and repeat the exercise every day for months on end, because life allows you that space. Great!

Go you!

I do highly recommend all humans, all ages, all genders, to heal. Three very different, yet very effective, retreats around the world specialize in supportive healing journeys. I am not sponsored by any of the below. However, I find them incredibly helpful, each in their own way. I do suggest these residential retreats to my clients, depending on which I feel best fits.

I, personally, have attended all 4 stages of the Path Retreats, and I have come out the other side as a new and better human. As of 2025, I am yet to return as a staff member to close the circle.

1. Path Retreats

A 7-day residential retreat with over 35 years of experience, facilitated around the world, specializing in mild and deep trauma release.

One of the most intensive and life-changing meditation and personal development processes in the world today, it has gained an extraordinary reputation amongst people who really want to come to know the truth about themselves. It is a profound inner work.

2. The Hoffman Process
A 7-day residential healing retreat with over 60 years of experience, that helps participants discover their true self, empowering them to create the life they want, the relationships they deserve, and a future that reflects their authenticity. Specializing in IFS (Internal Family Structures) resolving disruptive family histories.

3. The Diamond Approach
The fundamental practices of the Diamond Approach are designed to facilitate the radical shift to an intimacy with the totality of our experience spanning personality and Essence. This retreat will support your connection to yourself and to these practices, integrating and deepening of the sensing, looking and listening practice and your meditation practice – developing concentration, awareness and presence in an on-going way.

Kindness to self

How can you be kind to yourself if kindness is something you are not familiar with. Not because kindness isn't out there. But because you're not familiar with what kindness is, how it feels and how to detect it.

Right now, in this moment, please close your eyes and take a deep breath in. Hold at the top for one moment. Then sigh out. That was an act of kindness to Self!

Now, think of something you have done today. Anything that got you to the next thing. Let's say you made yourself a coffee, or you bought yourself a coffee.

Take a moment and say "thank you" to yourself. That was an act of kindness to yourself. You have looked after yourself, and you have met your **needs**.

You brushed your teeth, put on clothing, stayed naked − whatever it was you did. You did it because you followed what felt good. That was being kind to yourself.

Your system knows when it needs kindness or soothing and will act upon it,
no matter if you are mentally present with the action or not.
Now, practice becoming kind to yourself with intention.
I invite you to notice when you do things that feel good. Rather than randomly and impulsively reacting in a certain way, try to consciously create the moment.
Being kinder to Self also helps to energize your life more. See the following small increments of change you can make today for a better tomorrow.
When getting up in the morning,

- Take a moment to sit at the edge of the bed
- Allow yourself to take a deep breath before you get up
- Set an intention
- Don't look at your phone for the first 60–90 minutes
- Move or stretch for 10 minutes
- Have a glass of warm lemon water to wake up your gut and digestive system
- Don't talk to anyone for the first 20 minutes

- When taking a shower, don't just get wet but wash yourself like you'd wash a baby, be gentle, discover what feels good, and clean your skin.

There are scientific papers from around the world correlating washing your body with cleansing your soul. In fact, for as long as I can remember, I loved to take showers when I was in great discomfort. Eventually, I came to understand that it is my self-soothing mechanism. When I am sad, I take a shower to wash off the sadness. When I am angry, I take a shower to wash off the explosive energy. When I am in an argument with my beloved partner, I announce when I am too uncomfortable, walk away, and wash it all off.

Let's say you are at work, and a shower isn't possible. Remove yourself from the stressful situation for a moment, take a deep breath and wash your hands – if possible, splash your face.

How to practice kindness at home?

Wear that cozy jumper for three days in a row, have that piece of chocolate, and order that guilty-pleasure food once a month.

Now stop for a moment, and thank yourself for sticking around. This has been some seriously "tuff stuff" to read, but you are still here.

Give yourself a pat on the back – literally!
Put your right arm out and give yourself a pat on the shoulder for being here.

Now let's look at your self-talk. There can be these times when we are mean to ourselves. We often use worse language when speaking to Self, than we'd ever even consider using when talking to friends or strangers.
We curse, we disrespect, we shame, we shout, we belittle ourselves. Yet we'd never talk like that to our best friends, our siblings or co-workers, even our dogs.

So, what is it that makes us hate ourselves so much?

The good answer is, nothing. The bad answer is, everything we've learned as children.

To start being kinder to Self means we have to rewire our brains.

Good news, our brain is plastic. No, not the PVC kind of plastic. The neural-pathway forming kind of plastic, also known as **neuroplasticity**. Until the day we die, our brains are eager to learn and to physically change. We can – in the most literal way – rewire our brains any and every day of our lives.

The hard truth is, it takes discipline and practice.

Kindness is not something you can just go out and buy. Kindness is like a muscle. You cannot go up to a bodybuilder at the gym and ask him where to get the muscles, he'll laugh at you and point to the machines all around you. You gotta do the work.

Loving Kindness meditation

What if I told you that there is a "magic" meditation that will, over time and with regular practice, alleviate all your suffering and give you mental clarity. Its benefits include a longer life with less pain, better life satisfaction, improved relationships, and greater resilience.

No such thing, you say?
Wrong!

Loving Kindness meditation, also known as Metta, has been around for over 2,600 years. However, it's less commonly known than its highly misunderstood cousin, Mindfulness meditation. Find out more about all of the 7 ancient meditation types in my book *Meditation for normal people.*

Metta is also known in the ancient texts as Maitrī. Maitrī can be understood as loving kindness, friendliness, good fortune, good will, or benevolence. Metta is one of the 4 Brahma–

viharas (listed following), and one of the 10 Pārāmīs of the school of Buddhism.

4 Brahma-viharas

1.   Metta (loving kindness)
2.   Karuna (compassion)
3.   Mudita (appreciative joy)
4.   Uppekha (equanimity)

Metta has been studied by several universities around the world cooperating with Buddhist monks as their subjects. These included neurologists who observed them whilst conducting CT scans to measure their brain activity, psychologists who examined their behaviour patterns, and endocrinologists who investigated the hormone-balancing benefits, among others. Metta is backed by science.

Metta is a Buddhist practice that roots one's heart and mind in goodwill and universal friendliness toward oneself and others.
The above is achieved by directing particular phrases towards the Self, friends and/or family members, acquaintances, a person that has

wronged you, strangers and all living beings, one at a time.

These phrases are repeated while focusing on light and compassion at the base of your heart. They are either whispered whilst exhaling or said silently with your inner voice.

Most meditations that involve repetition of words, similar to a mantra, are chanted in Pali. Chanting is often mistaken for singing.

However, chanting doesn't activate the vocal cords for projection outward, but to evoke vibration and resonance inwards. When listening to the Tibetan Gyuto monks − famous for their chanting − even if you speak or understand Pali, you will at times have a hard time understanding a word, as these monks are not performing like a choir. These monks are dropping into a deep state of meditation by aligning their mind, body, spirit and breath with their chants.

Anyway, back to Metta. It also has a set of phrases that are to be repeated in a certain hierarchy. These can be fairly easily translated into English. Following is a guided Metta practice.

There are slight variants of this script out there, however, all forms of Loving Kindness meditation share the same goal of developing unconditional positive emotions toward all beings.

This includes feelings of:
- joy
- trust
- love
- gratitude
- happiness
- appreciation
- compassion

To practice Metta, you should be at home, or at a place that is undisturbed, safe and calm. A place you can easily return to, as meditation will deepen when practised on a regular basis in the same spot. You create an energy in that spot that which allow you to "drop in". Like muscle memory, once you are there, your body knows it's wind-down time and a safe spot to relax.

Metta should always be practised seated, **not**
lying down. The point is to be in absolute
awareness of your posture and your heart base.
Metta is best practised in the evening before going
to bed, as its properties allow for a shift in state
of mind, and aid deep sleep.

Once you have found your spot, get comfortable.
Set your space up for success. Make it cosy.
Maybe have some blankets around you, and a
couple of pillows to elevate your bum to avoid
cutting off the blood flow from your legs when
seated cross-legged. Perhaps some additional
pillows to support your knees if they cannot rest
on the ground. And you might want to have some
flowers or something similar to create a
welcoming environment. Find a sitting position
that you can remain in for about 20–30 minutes.
Refrain from using music as background, but
simply allow this meditation to be just you and all
the beings you send loving kindness to.

Once seated, straighten your back, rest your
hands on the upper third of your thighs, or in your

lap. Inhale deeply through the nose, and while exhaling gently, let your eyes close.

Take three deep breaths to ground in the space and in your body.

Start by relaxing your glutes and legs.
Relax your knees and feet.
Relax your arms, hands and fingers.

Now, relax your whole body, whilst still maintaining your posture.
Bring yourself to the present moment.
Establish your attention at the centre of your chest, the heart base.

Inhale and exhale deeply a few times, guiding your airflow through the heart base. Observe the lifting of the chest while inhaling, and notice the natural fall of the chest when exhaling.

inhale   exhale

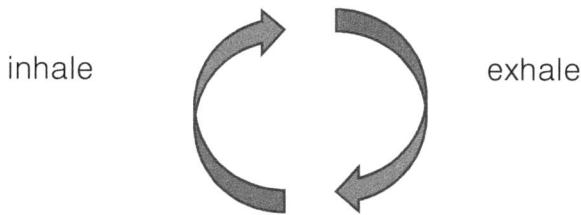

Let go of any concerns, commitments, or
responsibilities of the past and future.

Imagine the shining sun, radiating its light,
energy, and warmth in all directions.
The rays reach far and beyond, radiating to all
beings without prejudice, and without preference.

As to one, so to all.
Now, bring the light of the shining sun in front of
the centre of your body. Feel enveloped by the
warmth.

Bring the warmth and rays of the shining sun into
your body. Guide the sun and all its warmth to just
above your belly button.
Feel the warmth and tenderness.
Shine the light of the sun throughout your whole
being. Let the rays reach all parts of your upper
body, including the neck and head.

Follow the warm honey light rays bringing light to your shoulders, arms, all the way into your fingers. Have the shining light of the sun fill up your abdomen, every inch between your hips, down your legs, all the way into your toes.
Your whole body is filled with the white–yellow, warm, shining light of the sun. Know this light and warmth as loving kindness.

Your mind is filled with beautiful intentions, goodwill, best wishes, and happiness for yourself.

Fill your whole body with light and love.

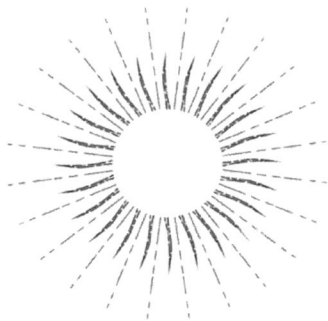

Now, move the shining, radiating sun itself up into your heart. Fill your heart's every chamber with warmth, tenderness and light.

Fill your heart with love for yourself – radiating and filling your whole body with goodwill and kindness.

Keeping your awareness at the heart base, and with full intention – really meaning it when saying it – repeat these words with your inner voice.

> May I be happy and well.
> May I be safe and warm.
> May I be far away from troubles and
> dangers.
> May I not be parted from the good fortune
> I have attained.
> May I be free from suffering.
> May I live happily in peace.

Remain here for about a minute and drink in all that is love.

Now, bring up an image in your mind's eye of your guardian – your parents perhaps, or grandparents, or an important teacher or mentor of yours.

Fill your heart with loving kindness and shine it toward them.
You have gratitude, love and respect for these important people in your life.

Keep your awareness at the heart base, and gently repeat in your mind.

> May you be happy and well.
> May you be safe and warm.
> May you be far away from troubles and
> dangers.
> May you not be parted from the good
> fortune you have attained.
> May you be free from suffering.
> May you live happily in peace.

Sit here for about a minute and shower all that is love toward these people.

Next, visualise a special person in your life. Maybe your partner or lover, your child/children, your sibling, or a close friend, perhaps.

Fill your heart with loving kindness and joy.
Rejoice in their successes and happiness.
Be happy for when they are happy.

Maintaining your awareness at your heart base, repeat with your inner voice.

> May you be happy and well.
> May you be safe and warm.
> May you be far away from troubles and dangers.
> May you not be parted from the good fortune you have attained.
> May you be free from suffering.
> May you live happily in peace.

Fill your heart with love for this person, wishing the best for them.

Sit here for about a minute and shower all that is love toward that person.

This time, I'd like you to bring a difficult person before your mind's eye. Someone who may have caused troubles of sorts in the past. Someone who maybe has hurt you.

Keep your awareness at your heart base. Pay attention to the person only, **not** thinking about what they did, or what they said, or their foolish behaviour.

Just think of the person.

Establish your forgiveness for their actions, and let go through love.
Continue to maintain your awareness at your heart base, and gently repeat in your mind.

> May you be happy and well.
> May you be safe and warm.
> May you be far away from troubles and dangers.
> May you not be parted from the good fortune you have attained.
> May you be free from suffering.
> May you live happily in peace.

Forgive, and let go. Remove any ill will towards them from your mind and be free.
Sit here for about a minute and let go of this person in peace.

And now, think of the people who share your household or community. The neighbours that live right next door to you, and everyone down the road you live on.

Fill your heart with loving kindness, beautiful thoughts and goodwill. Thank them for their support, their encouragement and friendship.
Fill your mind with this warm, shining, radiant loving kindness, and send it to all your community members – shining in all directions.

Sit here for about a minute and envelop all these people in loving kindness.

Finally, expand your warmth and radiating light to all humans in your city, your county, your state, your country.

Expand your radiant light to all humans on your continent, your part of the world, your hemisphere.
Extend out even further, to the other hemisphere, and include all human beings on this beautiful Earth.

Meet them with gratitude and shine your light towards them.
Sit here for about a minute and radiate brightly to all these people in loving kindness.

With your awareness at your heart base, and all human beings in mind. Shine your bright white−yellow light to all beings on this beautiful Earth. All geckos and birds, all pets and livestock, all insects and mammals, all reptiles and amphibians. Embrace all living beings with loving kindness.

As before − so behind, as above − so below, and all around.
Bring radiance to all trees and mountains, all meadows and lakes. Meet the world and all its

bounty with loving kindness, gratitude and goodwill.
Radiate out from the pores of your skin.

Perhaps your breath can assist you.

As you inhale, you can repeat,
    May all beings be happy.

As you exhale, you can repeat,
    May all beings be free from suffering.

Generate your gift of loving kindness and compassion for the world – radiating out from the heart base.
Remain here for about 15 minutes and envision how the glowing, golden, warm sunlight and peace blankets the world.

Once concluded, you may want to write down three or more things you are grateful for, and write down **one** positive thing that happened today.

Try to keep this peaceful energy within you while getting ready for bed. Refrain from using any electrical devices till the next day.

If you'd like to further your interest in how loving kindness has been explored in different ancient cultures, the Yogic texts have a similar understanding known as Bhakti Yoga.
Bhakti stands for love from a broader, devotional base level. The Sanskrit word "bhakti" comes from the root "bhaj", which means to divide, share, partake, or belong to. It signifies a strong attachment, fondness, homage, faith, or love for something spiritual or religious.

Bhakti, or bhakti-marga, is considered a path or method of spiritual practice in Hinduism, alongside the paths of knowledge (jnana) and action (karma).
The most beautiful interpretation I have ever read to understand Bhakti has stuck with me since 2015.

I didn't come into your life to teach you.
I came to love you. Love will teach you.

Consequences

The biggest consequence of an unhealed childhood is a fucked-up adulthood. If you don't address it, it will address you, and it will play you like a puppeteer. The following list gives you a broad overview of the side effects of an unhealed childhood:

- Peter-Pan syndrome
- Party boy behavior
- Gambling affinity
- Anger control issues
- Sex and/or porn addiction
- Codependency
- Commitment issues
- Serial dating
- Overachieving
- Hyper-performing
- Lack of motivation
- Vindictive tendencies
- Drug and alcohol misuse/addiction
- Serial traffic offending
- Gaming addiction

- Eating disorders like obesity/anorexia
- Gender fluidity/identity confusion (huge prevalence in 2020+)
- Lack of sexual desire
- Trust issues
- Infidelity
- Violence
- Restlessness/nervousness
- Nonsuicidal self-injury disorder
- Religious extremism
- Narcissism
- Agitation/fidgeting
- Emotional dysregulation and the list goes on ⋯

Fundamentally, this leaves us with one observation only. Lack of mental equilibrium and bodily homeostasis.

We will always choose a familiar chaos over unfamiliar safety, until awareness comes into the mix. There is more about that in my book about a trauma-informed approach.

Now that I've possibly popped your bubble of being "normal", let's look into how we might be able to balance a life from here onward.

A great step I have learned from one of my teachers is to verbalize your life and challenges. Verbalizing in a literal sense – make everything a verb, including yourself. By verb-alizing yourself, you take away the rigidity of nouns and allow the freedom of action and change to play a role in your developmental path.

Here's an example. I am Caroline-ing through life. I am a fluid ever-changing being. Caroline-ing today will look different from Caroline-ling yesterday or tomorrow.
Caroline-ing today might be simply sitting on the couch and drinking tea. And tomorrow Caroline-ing might be getting up on stage and speaking to 1,500 people about the trauma-informed approach to somatic release. Neither is less worthy of doing, nor more worthy of praising. It's just happening.

Dealing with consequences can also have a different name. Words like "responsibility", or "accountability".
If these two words give you the shivers, well I am sorry to inform you, but you are likely a very unbalanced person and full of shit.

Before you jump out of your seat and call me rude and throw the book out the window and write bad reviews – hear me out.
Remember where we talked about language? Language has an impact. Because I used the word shit, and suddenly you feel accused, is a big telltale of unhealed stuff.

What do I mean by that?
Well, I invite you to sit back for a moment and reflect on a recent scenario. A traffic annoyance, a friend upsetting you, your partner "poking the bear" in you, just one recent example that comes to mind.

Let's go with the partner example, as most people will be able to relate, whether they are currently in a relationship or not.

Your partner does something to annoy you, you get frustrated, and the two of you eventually end up in an argument.

Are you prone to accuse or to proclaim?

Accuse:
"You did this ···, this is your fault ···, you are so ···, you, you, you ···"

Proclaim:
"I feel uncomfortable when this happens ···, I dislike when we get into this situation ···, I would like to make a suggestion based on what happened the other day ···"
Accusation is pointing the finger at everybody but yourself. Playing the victim and giving your **ego** a field day. You are taking zero responsibility for your emotional reaction to events that are happening around you.
Emotional responsibility is to be aware of one's reaction to things. Honestly observing the inner arousal, the blood boiling, the ickiness.

Accountability goes one big step further. When taking accountability, you are choosing to examine the last time you felt that way – and the time before that – and then going back to when you felt like that for the first time ever.

SURPRISE! – it very, very likely has absolutely **nothing** to do with your partner at all, **but** with the let down of your parent/guardian. When they shouted, when they neglected, when they expressed a lack of love, and when they instilled deep unworthiness within you.

Same fight, different reactions.
Accuse:
"You are the problem, I am the victim, everybody else is wrong, I am right, and you don't care."

Awesome! What did you achieve? **Nothing**!
You are hurting anyway, but now the people around you are potentially hurt by your action too, and will act upon it.
It's a self-fulfilling prophecy!

"I only ever meet partners that end up behaving like this, and then we clash, and then we break up."

What's the common denominator? YOU!

Proclaim:
"I feel hurt in a situation like last Sunday at that party. When you behave like that, it's a trigger for me and activates my old childhood wounds. Do you think we can find a solution that works for both of us? Thank you for understanding."

We have a **winner**! You are taking responsibility for how you perceived it in the first place. You are taking accountability for how to dissolve it shortly after the incident rather than building onto it. And you are avoiding an argument, with a solution approach.

Guess what, any half-decent partner will be wowed and will very much be open to finding a solution. Win-Win.

For the curious amongst you, there are multiple great studies done by husband and wife psychologists, John and Julie Gottman. I could recite all their work and still would not bring justice to their discoveries. I highly recommend going on a YouTube rabbit-hole adventure on a rainy Sunday afternoon and getting some tough-love truths.

The freedom we gain

Okay, this might be the most controversial chapter I have ever written, yet at the same time might just be exactly what you need.

In the mindfulness practices we learn around the world, the core aim is to dissolve into nothingness, losing your identity and attachments, thereby gaining freedom, bliss and equilibrium.

What if it's not all that hard?

Who am I?
Let's quickly take some jumps back to the start, and then see how this new human became You.

You are Jon Doe.
Says who?
Says your passport.
Why?

Because your passport carries the name your parents gave you. They labelled you Jon.

You are not born as Jon. You are born label-less. You are born as a human, as a blank canvas with the potential to live and thrive on this planet.

As a being with a developing brain and a hunger for knowledge.

But now, you are robbed of that blissful experience, because now you have been labelled – Jon. And your parents tell everyone that you are Jon. Now other people start calling you Jon as your brain develops. Soon, you are about 14 months old, and you start believing them. When someone says Jon, you look at them, they show satisfaction with your reaction, and reflect back affection.

Okay, so you take on the label Jon because the affection satisfies your core need for love.

But then you are 24 months old and you have done something that your parents don't like. They still call you Jon, you still react, but now they show dissatisfaction when you look at them, and no affection when you react to them.

Well that's confusing, isn't it?

You start to develop a mixed sense of Self, "I am a good Jon and a bad Jon."

And that continues till today, sitting here, reading this book. You have grown, and listened to the label Jon for all your time on Earth, and you now firmly believe that you are Jon. Also you are able to distinguish that there are other Jon's in this world. However, they are very different to you. At this point in your life, you don't question that.

So there are good Jon's and bad Jon's, both out there and within you.

Jon has become Jon because people have called him Jon all his life, not because he has **become** Jon.

Why did you stick with the name Jon anyway? Do you like being Jon?

I personally didn't like nor identify with my birthname at all. In fact, I was so stubborn on that matter that I changed my name when I was 12 years old and chose to be known as Caroline. I did so, because Caroline suited me better and felt more like me. At the time, I was not aware of any other particular reason.

Did my family take me seriously? Not at the time, but 30+ years later I am still Caroline, and eventually **most** of my family members have come around to it.

However, a few people in my family, who are so rigid in their programming, are holding on to that label I was given at birth, and have refused to acknowledge that I changed it when I was 12.

Their lack of acceptance and their hard-wired programming keeps them imprisoned within a single, and strict, narrative about life. In their lives, I will never be Caroline. They will never understand how colorful a world can be if only you let go of a programming you never chose to begin with, but which was put upon you.

So sad for them.

We have all been given a construct early on in life, of who and how to "be" which we then build upon as we observe and are impacted by the world around us. From this, we determine the nature of success, status, and supposedly what is right and wrong in life. We become a set of stories we have been told, which eventually are the same stories we ourselves tell others.

Who we are is not the "truth". We have become a set of myths. Anyone at any time can break away from these myths, stories and labels, and start over! It's just mind over matter. However, these stories are so deeply integrated into our concept of life that breaking free from them can make us look ludicrous in the eyes of others.

I may have unlocked a life-crisis in you with this chapter, but I am very happily embracing that role. I unlocked this life-crisis by myself around my 30th birthday. **The best thing** I've done for myself.

I looked in the mirror, questioned who I was, how I got there, and what is really the truth of life, etc.

The ultimate result of questioning my reflection in the mirror was quitting the life people knew me to have.

Selling everything I owned and finding out what I am really here for – even if that meant there is no reason at all and I might as well terminate my being. Sounds melodramatic?

Well, just a little.

It only sounds melodramatic if you are trapped in the narrative you have been fed since birth.

For me personally, it was the most liberating thing I could have done. The reward for that radical action was finding my reason, my purpose, my true Self, and realizing happiness lies in each and every moment. Happiness only ever lies in the present, the **now**, not in the past or in the future, not in a third party or a thing.

What I have done is fundamentally refuse my given identity, which, in part, I started doing when I was 12. But then I forgot about it again due to the system we are pushed through in Western society. I decided to rewire who I identify as – a soul in a human experience.

With that came a whole lot less sorrow, less materialism, less disappointment. More gratitude for the tough times and more joy during the good times. We need to return to being happy **now**.

Try to imagine your death, your non-existence – dissolve into nothingness within your being, and your doing. And then build from the ground up.

Start with your breath, then connecting to nature, and slowly, step by step, construct around you the world as you wish it to be.

How that played out for me, you can read about in my novel *Off I Go... from Media to Mindfulness*.

Bio-makeup

What does that even mean?

Let's start by looking at some of the components of bio-makeup individually. We have DNA, we have Astrology, and we have the relative "newcomer" of the theory of Human Design. Each of these influence you, your behavior, your development and your resonance/energy.

DNA is your genetic foundation of being, gained from your mother and father, plus some random mutations. Astrological makeup is also fixed, as it is determined by your time, place and date of birth. Thirdly, there is Human Design, which is a pattern mapping, also linked to your birth. None of the above can we influence – they influence us. But what they give us, as individuals, is a tremendous level of ownership of our lives. Each of us has a unique bio-makeup.

DNA

Our DNA comes through conception from our family bloodline, and influences our physiological makeup. Blood type, hair/skin/eye color, tendency to illness, longevity, height, bone density, intellect, and all other physiological characteristics. To a degree, it also contributes to our mental predisposition towards happiness, depression, and cognitive thinking patterns.

Astrology

Our astrological makeup has a huge influence on our personality. It is determined by the positions of planets and constellations, dominant in the skies at the moment of your birth, during our planet's unceasing journey through the cosmos. Stick with me for a minute, I know it sounds a little woo-woo, but I'll make a clear distinction between Horoscope and Astrology.

In short, Horoscopes are an interpretation of the potential effects of planetary movements in relation to the zodiac constellations, on your behavior and mood for a short period of time.

Astrology refers to energetical resonance you cannot deny. It's a characteristic that is unique to your developmental pathways, highly influencing your motivations and emotional responses.

Yes, it varies to a degree between male and female, and one's upbringing does have an influence, too. However, the easiest way to explain what I am alluding to is by looking at the moon [it's not a planet]. Because of the moon, our oceans have tides. High tides and low tides occur about every 6 hours and 13 minutes.

Since the average human body is made up of about 60% water, it is sometimes speculated that our bodies are also affected by these tidal forces.

A second example is the phenomenon of solar flares which produce dangerous emissions of high energy particles and radiation, although the Earth's inhabitants are largely protected by its magnetic field and atmosphere. Solar flares cause a dramatic interference with satellites, pose potential threats to astronauts, and have been known to affect electrical power supply over large regions.

Within our bodies we are, in the most literal sense, responding to planetary changes, due to how water and energy move around. Certain behavior patterns can ebb and surge throughout particular periods of a month and a year.

Below is a quick overview of the order of the zodiac signs (commonly known as birth signs) and their top three personality traits.

Aries
March 21st to April 19th
Rambunctious, loyal, life of the party

Taurus
April 20th to May 20th
Quiet, knowledge hungry, emotionally challenged

Gemini
May 21st to June 20th
Ambitious, mostly gentle, inquisitive

Cancer
June 21st to July 22nd
Tribe oriented, easily depressed or overwhelmed,
loving

Leo
July 23rd to August 22nd
Flamboyant, passionate, polarizing

Virgo
August 23rd to September 22nd
Perfectionist, high anger threshold, community
oriented

Libra
September 23rd to October 22nd
Diplomatic, harmonious, intelligent

Scorpio
October 23rd – November 21st
Determined, resentful, honest

Sagittarius
November 22nd to December 21st
Adventurous, poised, faithful

Capricorn
December 22nd to January 20th
Enterprising, critical, relentless

Aquarius
January 21st to February 19th
Impulsive, altruistic, unique

Pisces
February 20th to March 20th
Mystical, romantic, impressionable

Human Design

The third ingredient to the perfect cocktail mix that makes you, You, is your Human Design.

Human Design is probably the "youngest" of all life-alignment theories, yet for the past 30+ years also the most truthful and accessible one. The Human Design theory was "created" by Alan Robert Krakower in 1992. He published a book called *The Human Design System* under the pseudonym Ra Uru Hu. Krakower developed the Human Design System following a mystical experience in 1987. Human Design has also been described as a psychological counselling instrument and "a comprehensive and personalized map of your unique energy and life blueprint, guiding you towards self-awareness, personal growth, and empowerment."

Human Design combines various traditions and ancient philosophies to "mathematically" discover your personality type. Human Design draws its information from astrology, the I-Ching, Kabbalah and Vedic philosophy.

Based on Krakower's findings, it centres around the division of personalities into 5 energy types, referred to as signatures, claimed to indicate how an individual exchanges energy with the world. They are Manifestor, Generator, Manifesting-Generator, Projector, and Reflector.

Each comes with a specific description of when you're most productive, how you utilize opportunities (listed as a strategy), and a particular feeling that comes up when you're not in tune with your energy type (labelled as the not-self theme).

In the theory of Human Design, similarly to astrology, they look into the alignment of planets – "the stars you are born under" if you will.

The specific alignment of planets you were born into is used to create a diagram, or "bodygraph". The bodygraph shows the 64 hexagrams described in the I-Ching, at various locations on the body. Within minutes of exploring my bodygraph, I felt like I had been handed the manual to life.

Through Human Design, you will discover why you are the way you are, and therefore how to manage your life going forward.

That can include tools to function and thrive based on what gives you motivation and how you make decisions. You will be able to recognize a pattern in your life when looking at your approach to love, business, or ambitions. For example, you might learn that you are not too lazy or lack zest for life, but that these behaviours are what make you, You.

You just might be a type that likes a slow and safe approach to life – not a go-getter. Or you sleep better alone than with someone sharing your bed. These are not weird, just part of your bio-makeup. This personalized knowledge perhaps allows you to openly communicate with your partner why you want a two-bedroom house and to sleep separately – not because you love him/her less, but simply because you are "born this way".

New parents are highly encouraged to get a Human Design reading for their kids, that can aid them in raising the kids to their highest potential, dissolve unnecessary disappointments, etc. Imagine a world where we all live the highest version of ourselves. Human Design doesn't just map where the planets were in the sky when you were born, like a birth chart.

Human Design also identifies your dominant Chakras to create your personal bodygraph.

To understand Chakras better, refer to my book *Meditation for normal people*.

Human Design isn't the cheapest option to get to know yourself, however it is thus far the most effective tool I have found besides plant–medicine sittings, such as ayahuasca or peyote.

Check the appendix of the book for more information.

Forgiveness & ownership

Forgiveness is probably one of the hardest exercises in self-redemption. Again, I'd suggest starting with the outer world first before starting to forgive oneself. Forgiving someone else is only half the work. Yet, as suggested earlier in the book, working on oneself, being kind to Self, is so much harder. Hence, I invite you to start easily and only then begin to draw the circle in closer.

Start very easy — a friend was late to a meet up or pulled a no-show on you. You have been friends for a long time, and it really didn't hurt that much. There might have been a 10-minute disappointment, yet your friendship isn't chipped. Fundamentally, you already forgave them without noticing.
Go back to that moment and proactively say your forgiveness toward them. Set yourself and them free of that disappointing event.
Now, look at yourself and investigate why you were disappointed, which expectations weren't met?

Take a moment and observe where in the body this disappointment resides. Are your shoulders tense, is your chest tight, are your legs stiff, is your jaw rigid, are your hands clenching, is your tummy in a knot, etc? Sit with that search, and then sit with that discomfort for a brief moment.
When you've reached the moment of clarity on where the pain lives, say "I am sorry. I forgive you. Thank you. I love you." to yourself and to your body.
It may feel silly at first, but the reaction of your body will teach you to build trust over time.

Now, take a deep, purposeful breath in and then exhale fully.

Find words for that disappointment and say to yourself, "I forgive myself for having put trust in another person rather than myself."
Observe the shift in your body. Does a different sensation arise? Maybe a feeling of shame, some heat in your spine, a tight throat, a different kind of discomfort than before.
Observe that too, follow the sensation to where it is living in your body, listen to it.

Similarly to the way we did with our mini-me in the inner child chapters.

When you have arrived at the location in your body where this sensation lives, investigate when was the last time you felt like this. And then try to trace down when you felt like this for the first time in your life.

There is a beautiful saying, by Lewis B. Smedes, in his book *Forgive & Forget: Healing the Hurts We Don't Deserve*

> *To forgive is to set a prisoner free,*
> *and discover that the prisoner was*
> *you.*

This is just so on point!

However, to forgive oneself means to own all your mistakes. Remember the thing about responsibility and accountability in the chapter Consequences? For how you dealt with a situation, and/or how you hold grudges in your life.

Example.

You grew up with abusive and/or neglectful parents. You are in your late 40s now, and you have a trail of failed relationships due to neglectful behavior towards your partners and a potentially short temper.

The common denominator in these relationships is **you**, not your parents. Your parents are the root cause of your initial misguided set of values, and they may have instilled certain behaviors in you. However, you are now a grown person and you have been exposed to many other humans around you. You have learned from films, media, friends, co-workers and society in general that your parents were not ideal role models.

Now it's on you to take accountability for your own shortcomings, forgive your parents for theirs, and start working on **your** current behavior. Taking responsibility for your behavior patterns means seeking support to overcome your misguided values. A therapist or allied-health professional will have all the tools you need to learn to forgive yourself.

The next time you start dating someone and you have a blow at them, catch yourself. Stop midway and rephrase.

"I am sorry, I didn't mean to behave like this. I am working on my behavior patterns. Let me get back to you when I am less enraged." – Move away from the situation.

Then look at your progress. Instead of beating yourself up or numbing yourself with a substance for having glitched, acknowledge the small but relevant step of having caught yourself and stopped before it got worse.

Then, sit with yourself, do the body check – where does the anger live, when was the last time you felt that way, when was the first time you felt that way. And then forgive yourself.

Practice creates masters. In a few years, you will be the person that people want to have around, because you are aware, mindful and kind to Self and others. Bingo!

Kindness to Self

It might be helpful to think of situations in life where you have been hurt badly. Picture up to three different scenarios that have occurred over the span of your lifetime. Take a piece of paper and write them down.

However, don't just write them down with a **normal** pen. Get some **color** pencils out, or crayons from your kids, or highlight pens. Write the scenarios down in the color that feels most connected to that particular situation.

Then take a red pen, even if you have just used it already, and write all three scenarios again, with the red pen.

Place the pen down, turn the paper over, stand up.

Take a deep, controlled breath in through the nose as deep as possible.

Hold on the top for the count of 4.

Exhale through the mouth for as long as possible till all air is released from the body.

Suspend at the bottom of the breath for the count of 4.

Repeat that cycle twice more.

Return to your normal breath, whatever that means for you in the moment.

Sit down again, turn the paper over, take a green pen and write the exact same scenarios again with the green pen.
Then, continue with the green pen and write next to each scenario:

"I forgive you [name of the person involved]."

Place the pen down, turn the paper over, stand up.
Take a deep, controlled breath in through the nose as deep as possible.
Hold on the top for the count of 4.
Exhale through the mouth for as long as possible till all air is released from the body.
Suspend at the bottom of the breath for the count of 4.

Sit down again, turn the paper over, take a blue pen and write the exact same scenarios again with the blue pen.

Then, continue with the blue pen and write next to each scenario:

"I forgive myself. I am sorry for having carried this issue for so long. I set myself free now and forever. I am at peace."

Put the pen down. Take a deep breath, and sigh out without holding. Take the piece of paper and crunch it, bunch it, rough it up into a tight ball. If it is safe to do so, burn it in an open space away from danger, children or animals.
Or chuck it into a shredder.
Or simply bin it outside of your house.

Forgiveness is a continuing exercise and often needs to be repeated multiple times. It works faster when combined with gratitude. Is there something for which you are grateful that was seeded by the incident.

May your peace grow beyond your grief.

A beautiful song to listen to, and observe what it evokes within you is, *Ho'oponopono* by The Emmit Sisters. Ho'oponopono is a Hawaiian practice of reconciliation and forgiveness. It means "to make right" or "to set things right".

It focuses on addressing problems in relationships, including with oneself, ancestors, and the world around us. The practice involves taking responsibility for one's part in any conflict and resolving issues through forgiveness, gratitude, and love.

Creation & curation

We have all been told from early on to create a meaningful life. But what does that actually mean?

There are many books written on "how to", but why does it seemingly never work? Well, there are two answers to that. One, because just reading a book is never going to change anything. Yes, you read that right. Even this book here won't change a thing if you are not ready to **choose** change.
Secondly, there is no incentive after having finished a book. So, if you **really** want to change, get a life coach or a friend to check on your progress and hold you accountable to the change you want to create.

Let's come back to the word create. What are we creating? A routine? A lifestyle, a way of life – is there even a difference? YES, THERE IS!
In this book I am defining the term "lifestyle" as a powerful extrinsic motivation you submit to by wanting to blend in with your supposed peers, to

run with the sheep, be part of the current movement referred to as "in", to be stylish, to not be out-standing.

A "way of life", in this context, is a proactive, intrinsic choice to pursue a living, creating routines that serve your best interest, yet may be contrary to the broader movement referred to as "in" by societal norms at the time. To truly be **outstanding**.

A dictionary definition:

Creation [kree a'shun] The action or process of bringing something into existence.

When googling "creating a life for yourself", the below come up as suggestions.

1. Begin the journey of self-discovery.
2. Learn to be happy with who you are.
3. Check in regularly with your self-talk.
4. Align with your personal values and morals.
5. Learn how to live in the moment.
6. Observe your thoughts, feelings, and memories.

As part of creating your way of life you have picked this book and read all the way to this page, so you probably know all of the above, or at least have heard of them.

So, how is any of that different from **curating** your life?
What does that even mean?

Well, to create kindness in your life, curation of your life is almost inevitable.
A dictionary definition:
Curation [kyu ra'shun] The action or process of selecting, organizing, and looking after the items in a collection or exhibition – or perhaps life itself.
Curating your life is looking at life in two ways. One is to selectively add new things to your life. That can be routines, that can be people, news outlets, social media channels, etc.

And second, it most certainly means to have a good, hard look at your life with a great level of detachment, subtracting what doesn't serve your highest good. Eliminating bad influences in your life will automatically shift your state of mind, creating clarity and room for inner peace.

By **creating** room for inner peace, and **curating** what will reach you, influence you and guide you, you will feel more **contented**. When feeling more content with life, you are calmer. With more calmness in your life, you are less aggravated – which equals kindness.

Ta Dah! Full circle moment.

Things to look at when curating your life.
Start with the immediate distraction. What social media channels do you use? Facebook, TikTok, LinkedIn, YouTube, Instagram, CacaoTalk, SnapChat, WeChat, QQ, Pinterest, Reddit, Rumble, OnlyFans, etc?

Look at the material presented to you on those channels. Let me take a wild guess – all rubbish? Maybe 10% educational and 5% inspirational. But when you are fully and truly honest with yourself, how much of these "life hacks" do you actually apply in life? Let me have another wild guess — none?

Okay, just for the sake of it, delete two of your social media apps from your phone for 48 hours. While these apps are gone, observe your withdrawal — it's real, trust me!
Equally, I invite you to observe what else you do in that extra time you gain while not doom-scrolling. In fact, before you delete the apps, screenshot the one or two best life hacks you have saved and finally try them in real life.

The next obvious action is to have a good look at your news intake. Do you have news apps, and do you have your notifications on for them? What kind of news apps are those? Are they reliable sources, with authentic and independent journalists, or are you hooked on clickbait culture like Daily Mail and Channel 7? Curate your news provider — AND — undo your notification settings! Schedule a time of day when you **want** to get the news in **bulk**. Don't get drip fed and ripped out of your life every 5 minutes, being sucked in and controlled by the apps, but choose to control the rhythm of your life.

You'll see how much more productive you become after just one week.

To conclude this book, the invitation is to start small. Start with where the book finishes. Erase some of the stimuli to your brain, and you lower your stress level. With a lowered stress level, you will be more alert in real life, noticing things you never noticed before. You will have more time on your hands when scrolling less. Bring in some more mindfulness practices like meditation or other physical outlets, like painting, hiking, yoga, or playing an instrument. Participate in the world around you. You will be enabled to witness acts of kindness all around you, which will have you become kinder to others in turn – and to yourself. With more kindness to yourself, you may feel curiosity towards yourself and start to look into connecting with your inner child or getting your Human Design graph. Your sleep will improve significantly, which will allow you to be more present and therefore calmer when awake.

Let's make the world a kinder place, one person at a time. It starts with you and, one person at a time, we can change the world within **this generation**.

With loving kindness,
Caroline

Appendix:

Prefrontal Cortex explained

Retreats:
https://pathretreats.com/
https://hoffmanprocess.com.au
https://diamondapproach.com

Peter Pan Syndrome

DNA explained

https://www.astrology.com/us/home.aspx

https://www.myhumandesign.com/

https://en.wikipedia.org/wiki/Human_Design

Ho'oponopono story

Ho'oponopono song

www.ingramcontent.com/pod-product-compliance
Lightning Source LLC
Chambersburg PA
CBHW070332090426
42733CB00012B/2457